Self-Control Skills at Home for Kids

*Fun and Entertaining Activities for Kids to overcome
Stress and Learn Self-Control at Home*

By

HNM Books

Self-Control Skills at Home for Kids

TABLE OF CONTENTS

CHAPTER 3: "LET'S DO SOME STRESS-RELIEVING ACTIVITIES" 44

Self-Control Skills at Home for Kids

CHAPTER 4: "SOME FUN AND EXCITING ACTIVITIES FOR SELF-CONTROL" 66

CHAPTER 5: "BECOME AWARE OF THE REALITY" 74

Self-Control Skills at Home for Kids

Self-Control Skills at Home for Kids

Introducing the Book

Does your child quickly become enraged when someone doesn't agree with him?
Does your child quickly become annoyed?
Does your child find it difficult to restrain his feelings when he is under stress?
Does your child easily become worried over insignificant things?

If so, this book is unquestionably for you. What is self-control in reality? It is described as the capacity of somebody to manage their feelings, passions, and choices in order to get advantages later. It's also important since it directly impacts a person's ability to achieve his objectives in life. For various people, success can mean a variety of things. Unquestionably, one important factor is self-control.

Despite appearances, most children lack self-control in certain aspects of their lives. For example, a child who struggles with self-control may appear to have everything he needs, but in reality, he struggles to complete his daily homework assignments on time and loses valuable sleep as a result. It is indeed important to recognize that aggressive behavior isn't necessarily associated with a specific condition. Impulsivity, for instance, is a hallmark of the *Intermittent Destructive Disorder*. This syndrome is characterized by outbursts of unjustified rage, where people may lose control and break in anger. However, those who are undiagnosed can also experience irrational hatred and rage. Another characteristic of binge eating disorders is impulsivity.

7

The significant difference between what young children are capable of and what they desire to do frustrates them. They frequently throw tantrums in response. Divert your child's attention with games or other diversions to try to stop tantrums. Try giving toddlers of two years old and above, a short break at a specified location, such as a wooden stool or staircase, to highlight the repercussions of outbursts and to educate them that it is preferable to go off by oneself rather than having an outburst. Children are better equipped to comprehend the concept of repercussions as they start school and the fact that they have the option to behave well or worst, both. Consider a red signal that needs to be followed so that your youngster can consider the issue before reacting. Help your youngster to cool off by leaving an unpleasant situation for a while rather than exploding.

Typically, older children are more aware of their emotions. Help them to consider and then examine what is making them lose control. Demonstrate how mostly, distressing circumstances aren't as bad as they initially seem. Encourage kids to pause and consider their options before acting. Let them see that their anger is caused by their thoughts about the problem, not the actual circumstances. Praise them on practicing self-control. Every child experiences stress from time to time. Stress is a common reaction to changes and difficulties and they are always going to exist, right from the early life. We frequently believe that stress is a terrible thing brought on by negative circumstances. However, anticipating happy occasions can sometimes be stressful.

Self-Control Skills at Home for Kids

Whenever there is something that needs to be anticipated, modified, or protected from, children experience stress. Whenever anything important to them goes at risk, they become anxious. Regardless of whether a change is for the best, stress is frequently the result. As a parent, you don't have to worry about this anymore. You will learn about a variety of techniques and exercises for reducing stress and gaining self-control in this book.

In 1st chapter, you will know the tips and parent's role in developing self-control in their children. The 2nd chapter describes the causes of stress and quick and effective tips to overcome stress in kids. The 3rd chapter entails some stress-relieving activities. The 4th chapter contains fun activities for self-control, and the last chapter unveils the techniques for self-control specifically designed for kids to practice at the ease of their homes.

Self-Control Skills at Home for Kids

Chapter 1: "The Best Warrior Never Gets Angry"

Kids do not simply begin to learn how to manage their urges and feelings. Until they are between 3 and 4.5 years old, and even after that, they continually require a lot of assistance. The authority on your kid is you, yourself. We know a lot about how kids develop. We are all involved in this. Why do kids lack in self-control so much? Kids under the age of three lack adequate brain development. Due to this, children are significantly inclined to act on their impulses, such as snatching a toy from a sibling's hand. In fact, according to a national parent survey,

10

parents reported higher expectations for their children than what those children are actually capable of exhibiting in terms of self-control, in response to being questioned about what age kids can withstand parental disapproval.

> *57% of Parents reported that kids could achieve this before age 3.*
> *According to 43% of parents, children could do this at age three or older.*

Once your goals for your child are in accordance with their capabilities, life for them will be significantly less frustrating. Knowing that your kid is expressing his age, that he requires assistance learning to control his urges, and that, despite how it may feel, he is not intentionally "badly behaving" can be relieving.

A variety of circumstances may influence a specific child's issues with rage, impatience, and violence. Anger is a common trigger whenever youngsters cannot receive the attention they desire or are required to perform a task that they may not feel like doing. Anger problems frequently coexist with other difficulties of mental health in kids, such as ADD, ADHD, Obsessive-Compulsive Disorder (OCD), and Tourette's Disorder. Anger and violence are assumed to be influenced by biology, including genes. Additionally, the environment plays a role. Trauma, dysfunctional families, and particular parenting practices also increase a kid's likelihood of displaying rage and violence that disrupts daily life.

11

Moreover, kid's anger has been linked to a wide range of detrimental effects. Violence, sadness, and medical problem brought on by a strained immune response are a few of these. Children who deal with their emotions incorrectly are in danger of dysfunctional interpersonal interactions and unfavorable results, including psychological and general wellbeing. These issues may persist into adulthood if a kid does not learn how to control their anger or build coping mechanisms. The most severe effects of child abuse are often the subject of school-based initiatives. Aggression management is a significant foundational element of these programs. However, these programs fall short in providing assistance to kids who don't exhibit aggressive characteristics and are introverts. Even if preventing violence is essential, it is insufficient to address children's rage.

My sister's friend once shared her story with me. She had 2 kids, and one of her kids had ADHD. Due to this disorder, he lacked in self-control. When she and her husband first discovered this, they were very terrified about how to grow their child into a responsible person. They tried many techniques to slow down the aggressive behavior of their child but all in vain. His behavior in school was not acceptable. Teachers complained about him frequently. She was very much depressed about her child's future. After some time, when she contacted me, I suggested her to read about this issue as much as she could and get her concepts cleared to overcome her fears and work practically for her child's betterment. She was very satisfied after the counselling and reading all the material that I could provide her. The couple applied the strategies and activities at home for their kid. It took time, but eventually, they were able to overcome their kid's aggressive behavior.

Self-Control Skills at Home for Kids

1.1: Evolution of Self-Control

According to new research, human self-control emerged in our ancient ancestors and was particularly noticeable approximately 500 million years ago as they learned how to construct complex tools. Although early humans like *Homo Erectus* could make simple hand axes as earlier as 1.8 thousand years ago, our human predecessors kept making more complex and carefully crafted variations of these weapons.

Self-Control Skills at Home for Kids

Furthermore, a child experiences a great number of growth processes as they progress from childhood into adulthood. Every one of these stages in a kid's development is characterized by unique, visible, and well-defined modifications in the children's physical, mental, intellectual, relational, and ethical spheres. Self-control development is one of these modifications and is a necessary step toward maturation and ethical adulthood.

It should be obvious mentioning that we shouldn't expect a child to exercise self-control since he lacks many of the necessary abilities at much younger ages. Self-control gradually improves with maturity, with some notable, significant changes occurring between the ages of three and seven. There is a great deal of personal diversity here as well, similar to other aspects of growth. Some children do struggle with self-control even at much older stages, which imparts significantly negative effects.

1.2: Develop Self-Control in Kids

Evolution, are you trying to listen? Self-control requires time to develop. Below are some effective actions you can take to develop self-control in kids.

- *Give Them Chances to Take the Leadership*

Give them situations when they must choose between using discipline or yielding to temptation. Tell your children that you will increase their pocket money by contributing to their accounts

14

when they achieve a specific goal. Graph their progress toward their objectives to let them see where they stand.

- *Maintain a Stress-Free Lifestyle for Them*

The brain, which acts as a stopper for the aggressiveness, reflexive behaviors generated by the hindbrain, is where self-control originates. For this reason, exhausted, overworked, unhappy, or worried kids could "break it." If you anticipate them encountering a situation that would challenge their self-control, assist them in developing a strategy while they are composed. Communicate with them regarding this before you leave if, for instance, *"when you are going to the convenient store, you can tell that them that they may be in for the visit and that they could come across something wonderful that they really desire, but now we're not going to buy any more toys or snacks, okay? I have no doubt that you'll make wise choices."*

- **Stop Stressing if Things Don't Always Go as Planned**

Kids are exploring with their ability to think and act independently. This is fantastic. Don't stress if they might not always strike the mark as much as the limit is set. With continuous exposure to stimuli, the brain adapts. They will develop self-control to a greater extent with more opportunities to exercise it.

15

Self-Control Skills at Home for Kids

- *What Advice Would You Give to Yourself?*

Any moment you can get kids to slow down long enough to start planning for the future, kids are putting more brainpower into that portion of their brains which controls impulsive behavior. Allow them to consider various consequences that could result from their decisions.

- *Home Chores*

Children will gain so much knowledge from performing routine home tasks. While having fun is crucial, there are times when you need to finish the difficult tasks first. Self-control entails the ability to put off the enjoyable activities until after the urgent tasks have been completed. They can test this out through the opportunities offered to them by assigning certain duties. Several of their chores should be rewarded for, and some should be considered part of their usual household effort.

- *Establish Limits*

Boundaries offer chances to practice self-regulation. It is nearly hard for children to know when to use self-control in the absence of limits. They must be aware of the dynamics of the boundaries.

- *Show Them How to Divert Their Attention*

It might be quite challenging to settle for what you desire! Give people a chance to practice waiting techniques, but be honest

16

Self-Control Skills at Home for Kids

about how long it will take. Since they enjoy the feelings it gives them, young kids often give their wants more thought. The more they consider it, the further their ability to restrain themselves is challenged. Instruct them to focus their minds and attention on something else when they're waiting.

- *Encourage Self-Awareness in Them*

Your kid will have greater control over their behavior and greater self-awareness if you assist them in comprehending the factors that have tendency to impair their self-control.

- *Play Games*

Self-control occasionally entails a strong effort against a behavior. It has been demonstrated that playing games that let kids exercise, improve self-control.

1.3: Parents Role in Kid's Self-Control

17

Self-Control Skills at Home for Kids

Parents usually must understand that their kids are maturing in a different time than they themselves did. They anticipate immediate satisfaction. If your kids are displaying bad behaviors, you are certainly not alone. The fact that the outcome is not predetermined is excellent news. A part of the brain that doesn't fully develop until the mid-twenties serves as the foundation of the mental monitoring system. In other words, your developing brain can learn to control emotions and avoid distractions because it is flexible.

- *Firstly, Control your Own Feelings*

Your children pick up skills by imitating your behavior. Essential clues for their growth come from how you handle your feelings during a dispute and the language you use in your regular contact with friends and family. Therefore, the most crucial thing you can accomplish is to develop emotional self-control so you can demonstrate the benefits of remaining composed and taking charge of yourself and the issue to others.

- *Making Use of your Personal Experiences to Teach*

Keep in mind that youngsters follow what they observe. Use these instances as chances to explain the value of self-control to your kids. Tell them the reasons behind your decisions, their results, and any potential impacts on the community. Simple and direct statements like "*I prefer to consume filtered water over soft beverages because it satisfies my thirst and is healthy for my body*" might be used to make a point.

Self-Control Skills at Home for Kids

- *Create Age-Appropriate Habits*

Kids can benefit from routines in the development of self-control and responsibility. Begin with tasks, including tooth brushing right after getting up in the morning, prepping the bag for next day before sleep and cleaning hands and feet when stepping into the house, etc. Then move on to time-bounded activities, like restricting screen time, paying attention to lunchtimes, and sticking to homework sessions as the kids begin to recognize the idea of time. When a behavior starts on its own, the youngster has to exert less effort to avoid external disturbances.

- *Timely Reminders and Play-Along Activities*

According to studies, it's beneficial to inform young kids about our standards or goals right before each habit or activity. They can maintain their focus by participating in role plays or by having them imitate your statements. Reminders should be delivered often and frequently enough, especially for younger kids. For example, I would warn my kid a few times before changing the channel. To respond to your kid's initial denials, have a few prepared responses.

- *Modify How Objectives Are Perceived to be Valuable*

A child is probably less attracted to anything when it is viewed as less desirable or harmful. For instance, you may find it difficult to limit the amount of sweets that your kids consume. In this situation, explaining to them and assist them in visualizing how

19

consuming too many sweets could lead to tooth decay. This will probably help to reduce their desire to eat the next piece of candy. Perhaps a more effective way to convey the message would be to show them images of damaged teeth.

- *Lessen or Eliminate Temptation*

When encouraging the kids to perform what's needed is important, you can think about lowering or eliminating the temptation. You can separate them while they are arguing and assign each of them a task which they enjoy. By doing this, you redirect their attention to activities that inspire them. For this reason, whenever we go out and about, I usually bring coloring books for my kids. If you want to stop someone from binge eating, take the sugary snacks away from them or swap them with better options.

Children will be children, and they will frequently bumble, fall, and look ridiculous. Be gentle, offer instructions, and show sensitivity to their needs and desires rather than scolding them for their actions. Remember that every child is different. Although some kids are inherently better at exercising self-control than others, practically everyone can look for ways to simplify it. I'm aware that it's simpler to say than do. I have also experienced difficult days. However, because they constantly understand how to live, our kids need us to be there for them. They require our love and faith. To improve the effectiveness of your techniques for yourself and your child during this exploration process, breathe deeply and make adjustments. It will be rewarding.

1.4: 10 Tips to Develop Self-Control

When trying to teach children self-control, choosing goals is the most crucial thing to remember. It is generally a good idea to choose easy and short objectives and to focus on one objective at a time. However, several general methods frequently assist kids in developing self-control, such as:

- *Request a Break*

When kids feel furious or disturbed, encourage them to go for a break and leave the situation. Among the tried-and-true methods that really work is this one. Kids forget and apologize in a matter of moments, returning to inner peace and even feeling good after a pause.

21

- *Educate Children about Feelings*

Kids begin to learn self-control when they distinguish between emotions and actions. Make sure your youngster understands that while assaulting somebody or shouting is not acceptable, feeling irritated or angry about something is. Your kid will be better able to control her impulse as a result, and she will look for other ways to manage with the emotion instead of behaving rashly.

- *Encourage your Child to Practice Listening*

Children tend to act impulsively since they frequently do not follow instructions. They typically get up and start wandering even when you have finished speaking. Before allowing them to take action, getting their thoughts on what they observed can help you to teach children to pay close attention.

- *Give Rewards*

Rewards can greatly aid children's ability to learn and maintain self-control. Children are taught to make brief compromises to reap long-term benefits whenever they have a specific goal in mind.

- *Impose Penalties*

There must be a punishment for bad behavior in addition to

Self-Control Skills at Home for Kids

rewards for good behavior. Kids are more likely to act such that they can accomplish goals to avoid the possibility of punishment.

- *Instill Problem-Solving Techniques*

Children who acquire problem-solving techniques consider their options before acting. Instead of settling a kid's problems for her, teaching them how to look for multiple solutions is best. She will get the ability to analyze a situation, come up with ideas, and then put the best one into practice. This will stop her from retaliating impulsively in the future to any issues that may arise.

- *Create Household Regulations*

Your kids will be aware of what is expected of them if you establish clear guidelines in your home. To keep your kids less prone to violate the rules, make sure you clarify what happens when they do. Create structure and a schedule to reduce confusion and the likelihood of impulsive behavior.

- *Display Ethical Behavior*

Being a role model for kids is important because they learn more from you than from anybody else. Your youngster can learn to control impulsive behavior by using self-talk. You should also provide an example for others on how to wait patiently and respond to a scene of postponed enjoyment.

- *Engage in Specific Exercises Meant to Instill Self-Control*

With the use of specific activities created to teach and build self-control in children, families can even assist young children in learning self-control. Playing games that teach impulse control, with children is one of the finest ways to provide them with a pleasant approach to reducing impulsive behavior.

- *Promote Physical Exercise*

Healthy and active kids have a higher chance of controlling their urges. Kids have bundles of energy, and if that power is not properly expended, they are more inclined to behave without thinking. Encourage your kid to participate in physical activities so that she can use her energy in a sensible and healthy manner. Additionally, this will maintain her mental and physical wellness while also assisting her in the development of self-control.

The ability to regulate one's ideas, emotions, and behavior is among the most crucial duties of parents. This is because adolescents who do not learn this seem to be more likely to act aggressively, struggle in school, and encounter unfavorable life experiences due to numerous improper behavior issues. Parents should incorporate the self-regulation abilities they are teaching their children into their style of parenting. This will additionally assist you in learning a valuable skill to better yourself both physically and emotionally and serve as an example for your kids.

24

Chapter 2: "Self-Control is a Skill; Thinking Positively is a Mastery; Power is in Calmness"

Each parent hopes to bring up joyful and contented kids. Nobody desires a baby who is anxious but everybody is unhappy due to life tensions. Psychological stress can have long-term negative effects on a kid's health. You can grow a peaceful, happy child with some effort and lots of love.

Following are the seven suggestions for raising a calm baby:

Self-Control Skills at Home for Kids

- *Peaceful Parents, Calm Kids*

Majority of a child's feelings are learned from their parents. Emotional disorders in parents are associated with emotional difficulties in their kids. The majority of anxious kids do have worried parents. Your youngster will worry whenever you worry. Being a calm parent is indeed the best approach to raising a peaceful child.

Be at ease more frequently if you want your youngster to be more composed. Try to be encouraging and use good language. You'll be more composed by downplaying minor conflicts and using positive encouragement.

- *Never Overlook that you are Speaking to a Kid*

Children frequently act out in damaging ways, such as throwing tantrums. A kid lacks emotional maturity. Children do not get born with the knowledge and capacity to control their emotions. Anxiety results from treating kids like little, illogical adults. Parents need to quit analyzing their kids' motivations negatively. A bad action could be an effort to satisfy innocent desires.

- *Understand your Child's Needs*

Generally understood as they are able, parents should consider their children's wants and needs. Anxious parents are more concerned with their child's safety and well-being than they are with evaluating the truth. This results in stressing your kids.

Self-Control Skills at Home for Kids

Providing your kid what they genuinely need and addressing unreasonable anxiety and fear will help them feel more at ease and content. However, as new difficulties occur, take their demands into account.

- *Improper Expectations*

Everyone feels the weight of expectations. Unacceptable expectations for kids can lead to a variety of worries. Parents shouldn't project their children's future selves too far. Parents and children will both feel stressed as a result of this. A behavioral and emotional youngster may not always have the resources at their disposal to maintain calm; thus this needs to be taken into account. Your kid lacks the ability to maintain composure. Like anything else, this needs to be taught to them as well.

- *Encourage Techniques for Calmness*

Yoga for kids and meditation might help your youngster to relax. If they are frightened, teach children to start counting from 1 to 10. Your children will discover how to become a little bit more relaxed if you practice calming exercises with them.

- *Be Dependable*

Find the primary cause of children's tiredness and irritated self; food or sleep deprivation? A kid who is hungry and exhausted will be unpleasant and cranky. Organize your regular routines,

27

Self-Control Skills at Home for Kids

so it does not conflict with your regular nap or lunch times. If those same needs are not met, kids are more prone to experience anxiety.

- *Give your Youngster Some Control*

Allow your youngster to develop emotional self-control. Stress might result from failing to acquire new skills and take on additional responsibility. A kid has something fresh to learn each day. As a result, your kid will become a more independent and composed young person.

2.1: Why do Kids Lose Control?

The days when kids were "watched and not allowed to speak" is over. Parents these days are aware that a kid should be able to

Self-Control Skills at Home for Kids

exhibit a variety of emotions. However, parents may find it difficult to guide their kids in controlling strong emotions. Avoiding yells in the chocolate section is only one aspect of being able to control your emotions. It means learning how to manage irritation, deal with failure, self-soothe under pressure, and ask for help from family members or friends when necessary.

Teaching kids to understand the indicators that someone is likely to lose control is a good starting step for parents. Do their breathing and heartbeat become more rapid? *"Express how breathing exercises help people to settle down to a bearable level so that their mind can assist them in coping."* Parents can encourage kids to deal with their emotions, tell them that these emotions are natural, and provide coping mechanisms like playing outside or counting. A parent must step in and set clear boundaries when a kid acts out rather than controlling their emotions, such as, *"If you threw something at your friend again, you will be forced to go back to your room."* Consider these rules for developing discipline in your child.

- *Establish Guidelines and a Framework*

Unbelievably, children enjoy boundaries and restrictions. When children believe that their families can set and enforce rules, they feel secure. These tactics can be useful if you have trouble in getting your kids to pay attention.

29

- *Clarify House Regulations*

By establishing a detailed, documented set of rules, chaos can be decreased. Pay attention to fundamental guidelines like *"Use polite language"* and *"Ask before taking anything."* Once they are spelled out in writing and acknowledged as a family, rules are easier to uphold.

- *Make a Framework*

Increase the amount of discipline in your kid's day to establish a routine for the entire family.

- *Assign Tasks*

It's crucial to give your kids regular age-appropriate activities so that they can experience being accountable. Additionally, get your kids accustomed to helping out.

- *Positivity in Language*

Consider your children's abilities rather than their limitations. Say, *"You may watch the cartoon as long as your room is neat."* Provide your youngster with empowering options that will give them some degree of control.

- *Give Directions that Work*

It matters how you provide instructions. Only deliver one instruction at a time and be strong and straightforward. Ensure

Self-Control Skills at Home for Kids

that your youngster is paying attention while you talk in a calm manner.

✓ *Deliver Repercussions for Bad behavior*

Clearly define the repercussions of violating the rules. Punishment should always be clear. Your kids are far less inclined to misbehave if they are aware that breaking the rules will result in instant punishment.

Time-out: In the past, a time-out was applied to deal with aggressive actions. A *"take it easy corner"* is a better remedy. It's crucial to provide your kid with the tools that they require to have for enhanced self-control. Instead, if they become poorly developed, they will revert to their previous behaviors.

Elimination of Benefits: This could involve taking away gadgets, a beloved item, or a pastime, but do not do it for an extremely long time. If parents completely remove incentives or withhold them for several days, your kid might lose hope or act aggressively.

Compensation: may be required if your kid's inappropriate behavior causes harm to another person. Tell them to compensate for the person they offended or give the individual their new toy. Help your child to develop the habit of accepting the consequences of their actions by enforcing logical reasoning.

31

2.2: Help Your Kid to Calm Down

Everybody, including children, is vulnerable to emotions. They occasionally lose control when they are irritated. Some kids don't understand how to deal with their tension and anger, which can result in emotional outbursts. This is where parents step in and help their children to learn healthy ways to express their emotions. Here are some suggestions for teaching your children how to stay calm:

- *Motivate and Inspire your Kid*

Except when their environment makes them uncomfortable, your kid won't become irritated. Ensure that they feel at ease and at home in order to prevent misbehaving. Keep your children close if you take them outdoors thus, they won't feel insecure when you leave them on their own.

- *Go for a Walk*

Taking your child for a stroll will help them defuse their energy. This activity is very beneficial, particularly for children with ADHD. Spend 5 to 10 minutes taking a stroll across your area. You can either speak or remain silent while walking.

- *Embrace Your Kid*

Occasionally, giving your child a hug will help them to relax. Whenever your kid is distressed, a hug always helps them feel

Self-Control Skills at Home for Kids

good. Giving your upset child a hug can help them understand that you appreciate them and will be there for them. Although no parent enjoys watching their child cry, tears are typically the symptom of an angry child.

- *Perform a Quiet Task*

Disciplining your kid in the midst of a crisis is not recommended. Allow your child to engage in a non-verbal activity to help them relax. Creating puzzles, watching a favorite movie, sketching, or painting can all be considered peaceful pastimes. These peaceful activities will keep their interest, which will enable them to calm down. Here are some examples of worksheets mention below:

Self-Control Skills at Home for Kids

Self-Control Skills at Home for Kids

Self-Control Skills at Home for Kids

- *Whenever your Kids Are Furious, Resist Trying to Control Them*

It's better not to try to manage your kid's reaction if they are sad or furious. They will fight back and become more irritated if you attempt to restrict what they should have been experiencing. This will eventually intensify the condition. Remain composed and avoid dominating them.

- *Create Bubbles*

Bubbles are a great stress reliever for children. For younger kids, it will be enough to let them observe and burst the bubbles simply. They can easily forget their irritation by engaging in this pastime.

- *Break for a Meal*

Give your youngster some juice and a meal to help them relax when they're unhappy. A youngster may become irritated if they are thirsty or starving. These things may affect a kid's emotional health. Parents are encouraged to keep an eye on their kids and comfort them with food.

- *The Key is Consistency*

If you do not really put these suggestions into constant use, they won't happen. Repeat these suggestions whenever they become irritated until you discover the best technique to make them feel

36

better. Children require ongoing coaching if they are to understand how to regulate their thoughts and emotions.

2.3: Stress does not Kill us; it is How We Respond to Stress!!

Today, everyone is under more stress than ever before. Our understanding of the world has drastically changed. As a consequence, the effects do not spare our kids even. Many children are currently having difficulty, just like adults. Kids make excellent "*Noticers*." *Have you ever caught your youngster repeating anything you might have said when you thought they didn't hear it? Have you ever been shocked when they brought up a subject you assumed they had no understanding of?* They take up on these conversations verbally. Additionally, they take up the emotions of others around them.

Kids can lack the mental awareness or words necessary to communicate their feelings. They also don't comprehend what is actually going on. They simply find it strange, unsettling, uncertain, and simply scary. Pay attention to their psychological or behavioral indicators to assist and direct them during these trying moments.

A kid's regular behavior can vary as a result of stress. Different age groups and stages may exhibit this differently. Common modifications include:

Self-Control Skills at Home for Kids

> *Being irritated or anxious*
> *Abandoning activities, they formerly found enjoyable*
> *Regularly expressing concern*
> *School-related complaints*
> *Screaming*
> *Expressing frightened reactions*
> *Getting too attached*
> *Affecting one's food and sleeping habits*

2.4: Causes of Stress in Kids

While most adults consider their early life to be their best period, kids and adolescents are also vulnerable to stress, which may worsen their temperament and lead them to anxiety. According to studies, social conditioning, anxiety about school, and a variety of other factors cause nearly one in four kids to develop anxiety before they turn 18 years old. Here are some of the causes of stress in kids:

- *Separating Stress*

Families, take note: For infants, children, and teenagers, separating stress can be a significant stress factor. While separation stress is frequently a normal reaction to becoming apart, it may also be a result of unrelated pressures, like a new babysitter. According to research, children's patience for other problems tends to decline when there is a source of stress. Excessive clinginess, difficulty in saying goodbye, or anxiety about just being separated from you might result from this.

Self-Control Skills at Home for Kids

- *Family Adaptations*

Kids of any age might experience stress due to significant family changes, including death, separation, and a parent losing their job, or moving away. Even the most emotionally at ease youngster may experience some tension due to the complexities of increased emotions, disturbing schedules, and unusual routines. Change can lead to stress. Stress might happen if a big change is made to how life has typically been.

- *School*

School can be a significant source of stress for kids and teenagers. Stress can be brought on by a child's feelings of anxiety about homework or academics, multitasking, difficulties with friends or harassment.

- *Extremely Full Schedules*

Kids like taking their time to observe the world they are in and living in the moment, thus overcommitting them to many activities or hurrying them from one location to another can lead to stress. A youngster may experience stress if a family's hectic schedule or to-do list ignores their routine.

- *Unanticipated Global Events*

Kids of all ages can be impacted by major frightful occurrences (such as calamities, terrorist attacks, and mass killings) or by

Self-Control Skills at Home for Kids

seeing violent behavior on the news. Your kid may be influenced by even unintentional access to a horror movie or television advertising. Children frequently absorb the tension they are exposed to. Pay close attention to any disturbing or violent images that are present in a child's life, and keep an eye on older kids' online activities.

- *Everyday Irritants*

A kid may become stressed out as a result of numerous minor stressful events. Furthermore, some youngsters experience daily pressures like hunger, neighborhood crime, family struggle, an absence or regularly disappointing parents or relatives who act negatively or dangerously.

2.5: 8 Steps to Help Kids to Cope with Stress

We develop coping mechanisms as we get older to deal with the stresses in our life. We must be able to instruct our kids to do the same. Educate them on a few short-term relaxing techniques. Children must be able to take action right away to defuse stressful situations. Your youngster needs a few basic strategies, so educate them on these.

- *Visualize your Preferred Location*

Ask your youngster to visualize their favorite location on earth. Perhaps it's at the seaside, in the forest, or a peaceful area of your house. Ask them to reflect on this location using their senses—

40

what are they able to hear and feel? They should be encouraged to remain there in their vision for a while.

- *Make your Schedule Simpler*

There is so much push to get out. The entire family is under a lot of anxiety as a result of it. Discuss your kid's routine with them. *Still, enjoy each of their actions? Do they have any habits they'd wish to get rid of?* Stress could be reduced by reducing out and about activities to just one or two per week. Reducing the schedule would also give everyone more time to relax and enjoy, which is a fantastic way to relax.

- *Discover Helpful Diversion*

There are occasions when you can take action to lessen stress, such as reducing your activity level. For example, when their grandma is ill, although there is nothing they can do, your kid may constantly think about it and they may not concentrate in class. The next step is to try to divert their attention from their tension.

- *Look for Something Funny*

Come up with some ridiculous jokes. Children who laugh can feel a little better and experience less stress.

- *Kindness*

Locate an area where they can help. Act kindly to people.

41

Self-Control Skills at Home for Kids

Concentrating on others can help kids forget about their problems.

- *Play a Game*

Take out your childhood favorite game to allow aside some time for it. Show them the game. What a pleasant method to develop a relationship with your child!

- *Appreciate the Smallest Victories*

When faced with a brand-new problem, the majority of kids experience some degree of anxiety but finally they jump in because prior victories boost their confidence. The same encouragement is required of children who develop and think in various ways, but the rewards are frequently more mysterious. Keep an eye out for chances to acknowledge successes. Your kid may have solved a couple of extra word puzzles without stepping off the table. That's a victory! It could be less intimidating for your youngster to take on new tasks if they know what it feels like to succeed.

- *Showcase Effective Coping Mechanisms*

We, as parents, are our kid's first educators. They observe our actions and responses while we are under stress. We also need to set an example of appropriate coping mechanisms. There will constantly be tensions, so how you handle it, is what matters most. The greater your kid's range of coping mechanisms will be;

Self-Control Skills at Home for Kids

the sooner you can teach them. They can successfully handle challenging situations if they have a solid basis of coping mechanisms.

Self-Control Skills at Home for Kids

Chapter 3: "Let's Do Some Stress-Relieving Activities"

Since they frequently lack the terms to express their emotions, kids often experience stress in differing ways than grownups. This suggests that stress can show up in several of ways, such as mood swings, irrational behavior; sleep problems or focus, and even headache or abdominal pain symptoms. Harmful habits like binge eating or addiction issues can also be brought on by stress and worry. Giving your child appropriate coping mechanisms for their feelings at an early age will equip them with the abilities that they'll need as they mature.

Getting regular exercise is one strategy to reduce stress and improve mental health. Discover the reasons for this and get suggestions for stress-relieving activities you can do as a family.

3.1: Practice Yoga

Yoga is a type of physical activity and meditation that is excellent for de-stressing and cleansing the mind. Similar to exercising, yoga might be beneficial for your youngster to practice before sleep and after getting up in the morning. It can be beneficial to have a peaceful mind to begin the day.

Below is a series of yoga positions that you can practice with your children to reduce stress. To generate a yoga "rhythm," steadily perform each exercise one by one. Help your child to perform these positions.

Swan Dive: Place your feet apart when standing. Pausing for a breath, extend both hands to your shoulders and toward the sky. While maintaining a correct posture, steadily drop your hands and bend at the waist. Grab hold of the ground.

Downward Dog: Out from the swan dive, step your legs back into the downward dog position till your posture resembles the style of an "A." Put your hands on the floor.

Cobra: In the cobra position, put your arms apart and raise your shoulders until your spine is arched and your abdominal muscles are stretched.

Child's Pose: Knees should be apart as you force yourself to your palms and knees position. Lower your bottom to your feet while rubbing your big toes gently. Stretch your both arms as much as you can, lower your stomach between your legs, and place your head on either the ground or your palm. You can maintain this position for as long as you wish and then repeat the movements if you wish.

Self-Control Skills at Home for Kids

Self-Control Skills at Home for Kids

3.2: Make Puzzles

One amongst my favorite stress-relieving activities is a puzzle. They are appropriate for a variety of ages, especially adults, due to their great variety in terms of intricacy, size, and type. In addition to being essential in the preschool and primary school years, puzzles are equally required for the growth of kids of all older ages too. It is the best activity for reducing stress in kids. It helps parents get attached to their kids and engage them in fun activities. Puzzles foster a broad range of skills, which makes them the perfect academic play exercise for young children.

Self-Control Skills at Home for Kids

Self-Control Skills at Home for Kids

3.3: Aerobic Exercise

Another of the best methods to lower stress in kids is aerobic exercise since it can increase blood flow and release "feel-good" hormones. Enjoy one of the following fun family activities:

- ➢ *Riding a bike or a scooter*
- ➢ *Group picnics*
- ➢ *A dancing hoop*
- ➢ *Jumping rope*
- ➢ *Going for a swim*

Don't stress about wasting a lot of time on aerobic activity if your schedule is already jam-packed. Kids should engage in exercises

Self-Control Skills at Home for Kids

for a minimum of 30 minutes every day, but it's possible to divide this duration up into smaller chunks.

3.4: Dragon Breathe

Kids breathing cycle will modify when they are feeling stressed or anxious. They will start breathing quickly, shallowly, and rapidly, which only serves to heighten anxiety. Your kid can concentrate on a topic other than worry and anxiety by practicing mindful breathing, which involves inhaling gradually, holding the breath for a couple of seconds, and afterward slowly releasing out through the mouth. When their breath slows, your kid will feel more relaxed. The best activity for your kid is mindfulness breathing since it is practical and accessible whenever they need it. This is essential when you cannot assist with your kid's needs.

3.5: Art and About

Although it may not occur to you, kids can become stressed out just like everyone else. When unaddressed, these tensed emotions can lead to various other issues, including insomnia, excess weight, depression, and mood changes. Such problems may range from having homework to stress over to having trouble in social environments.

The good news is that creative activities have been shown to reduce stress and assist kids in letting out any bottled-up feelings they may be experiencing in their daily lives. A hormone normally linked to stress is decreased in the brain during

51

activities like sketching and painting, for instance. As a result, these pastimes can prevent the development of future mental illnesses like stress, sleeplessness, and anxiety. Below are some worksheets you can help your kid to draw on it.

Finish Drawing the Teddy Bear

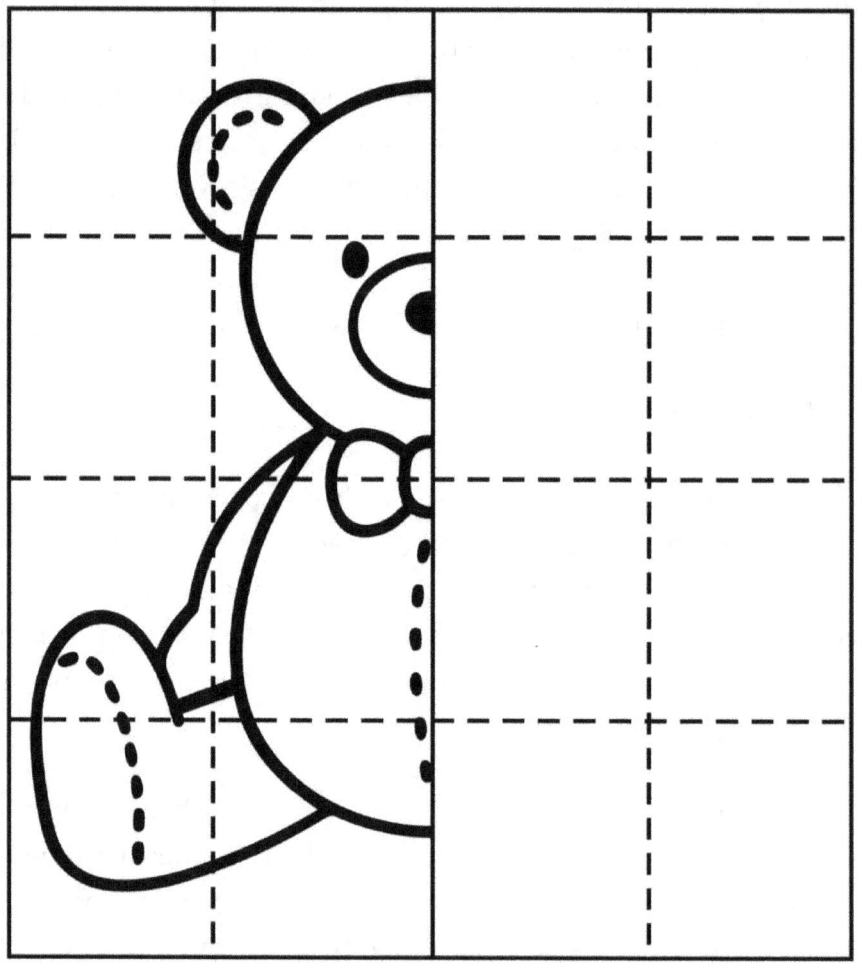

Self-Control Skills at Home for Kids

Turn these circles into anything you choose!

Self-Control Skills at Home for Kids

54

3.6: Play with Pets

Play with pets is one of the best stress-relieving activity to do with stressful kids. If you do not yet have a pet, I advise getting one just for your kid. Whatever you and your kid both agree on, it can be a bunny, puppy, or kitten. If not, let your kid see their pet-owning friends. Depending on their age, provide your kid the supervision of your pet or take good care of it yourself. The capacity of a kid to think about others and their points of view is improved by giving them responsibilities. They'll be ready to see

Self-Control Skills at Home for Kids

the opposing viewpoint. Their tolerance increases as a result, and stress gets reduced. Kids immediately forget their own worries when they are engaging with pets. This supports their physical and mental recovery so they can operate productively once more.

3.7: Get Your Hands on Cooking

The aroma of freshly baked cakes and desserts is irresistible. Unbelievable as it may seem, kids will like helping you in the cooking while preparing. Allow them to mix the bread or sprinkle some white chocolate on the topping. Since mixing the bread uses some energy, it actually helps kids release stress. This is very similar to the squeezing toys we use to relieve stress.

3.8: Do Some Gardening

Bring your kid to shop for seeds, soil, and a container. Allow your kid to get themselves a little filthy and dirty looking. Request that they daily hydrate the plant. You assign your kid this task in addition to others. Kids find peace in nature, so needing to grow a tree on their own is a whole new experience for them. Planting flowers teach tolerance and reduces stress. It is a skill that everyone should learn.

3.9: Create an Interesting Story

Creating an interesting story is a fun activity for kids to reduce stress. In this activity, you will help your kid to think about the main characters and build an interesting story. It can be very

Self-Control Skills at Home for Kids

exciting activities if you will help your kids. Below are some worksheets to practice this activity.

Characters

┌─ Title ─────┐ ┌─Author ──────┐
│   │ │   │
│   │ │   │
│   │ │   │
└─────────────┘ └──────────────┘

The characters are the people and animals in the story.

Who are the characters in the story?

- - - - - - - - - - - - - - - - - -   - - - - - - - - - - - - - - - - - - -

- - - - - - - - - - - - - - - - - -   - - - - - - - - - - - - - - - - - - -

- - - - - - - - - - - - - - - - - -   - - - - - - - - - - - - - - - - - - -

- - - - - - - - - - - - - - - - - -   - - - - - - - - - - - - - - - - - - -

┌──── **Draw a picture of the characters.** ────┐
│   │
│   │
│   │
│   │
│   │
└───┘

Self-Control Skills at Home for Kids

Story Time: Once Upon A Time

Complete the story.

Once upon a time there was a _____

who _____

One day, _____

At first, _____

After a while, however, _____

_____

Then, _____

_____

Finally, one warning, _____

_____

From then on, _____

_____

After a few months _____

_____

_____

We can learn from this story that

_____

_____

_____

Self-Control Skills at Home for Kids

3.10: Write in Your Diary

Not all children are capable of writing lengthy personal notes, and that's totally fine! It is intended to promote creativity and usually entails a child's summary of himself or about the day. In the first year, my child began keeping a sketch and writing diary, and it quickly became one of her daily favorites. The task was very open-ended, with the only "regulation" she had to adhere to was that each entry in her notebook had to be a complete phrase. Prior to entering grade 1, my child wasn't a great writer, yet by the age, she was in class 3 she had started writing full-length novels, and she now lists creative writing as one of her favorite kid-friendly stress-relieving activities. Turn over the page to find the template of diary writing.

My Day

Monday Tuesday Wednesday Thursday Friday Saturday Sunday

The weather today was: _____

My mood today was: ☺ _____

Today I: _____

_____

_____

_____

_____

_____

_____

My favorite part of today was:_____

_____

_____

_____

_____

_____

Tomorrow I want to:_____

_____

_____

Self-Control Skills at Home for Kids

3.11: Play Board Games

A board game with friends is the best way to decompress. Instances of relaxing board games are jigsaw puzzles and Sudoku, which are also old classics. You can also calm and enjoy yourself by playing cards or chess.

3.12: Straw Painting

Kids' stress-relieving activities that allow them to concentrate on their breath are among the best. A youngster naturally brings himself back to a moment of peace by taking long, deep breaths. Making creations with straws is a fantastic method to accomplish this with your children. Simply sprinkle some puddled watercolors paints on paper and instruct your kid to blow hot air through a plastic tube to spread the paints. It's easy, enjoyable, and great for helping youngsters to feel calm.

3.13: All About Me

Perhaps one of my favorite notebooks for kids would be one that you fill jointly if you're searching for a method to bond with your children while simultaneously teaching them the value of consistently managing stress. You can find a ton of these on the internet. They give you amazing chances to talk with your kid about various interesting subjects to let you know each other a bit more. It includes writing about yourself and your personality, etc. You can help your child in this activity. The following page

Self-Control Skills at Home for Kids

contains a workable example of this activity which you can help your kid to do.

All About Me

My Name is

I am [ ] **years old**

My Photo

My Friends Name is

My Favourite Color is

I love..........

My Favourite Food is

Self-Control Skills at Home for Kids

All About Me

My name is:_____

My favorite subject is:

I prefer to work:
- Alone
- In a Pair
- In a Group

● ●

School is fun when...   School is hard when...

● ●

Outside of school, I like to:

Self-Control Skills at Home for Kids

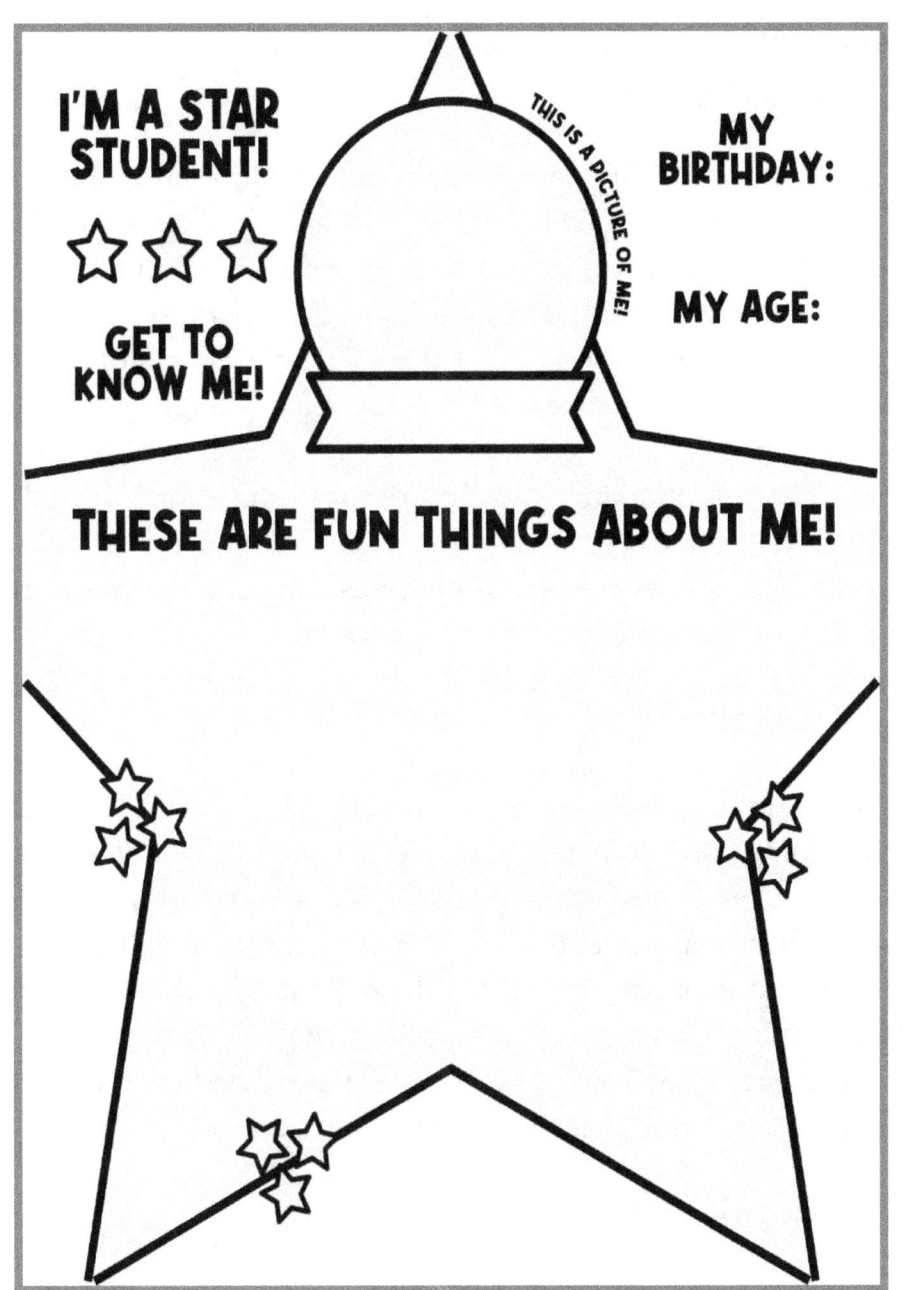

I'M A STAR STUDENT!

GET TO KNOW ME!

THIS IS A PICTURE OF ME!

MY BIRTHDAY:

MY AGE:

THESE ARE FUN THINGS ABOUT ME!

Self-Control Skills at Home for Kids

Chapter 4: "Some Fun and Exciting Activities for Self-Control"

Our capacity for self-control allows us to pause and consider options before acting. This entails pausing when our emotions threaten to take over in order to process the circumstance, evaluate potential solutions, weigh the repercussions, and proceed with the best course of action available. For children and young people, self-control is an especially tough executive functioning skill, and there's a scientific basis for that. Our brain, which controls thinking, resisting desires, and exercising self-control, develops later in life and is in charge of controlling emotions. Simply expressed, this implies that young people need to practice their self-control techniques a lot.

4.1: Tap Balloon

Balloons and a large area is all that is required for this entertaining game. Ask the kids to form a circle and divide them into two teams (A & B). Balloons should also be arranged in a circle. Select team A and team B. Firstly, team A will tap the balloon and then team B will tap the balloon in next turn. Both the teams have to be careful. Continue switching them every 20–30 seconds. Kids will have to pay close attention to hear the audio signal that indicates when it is their group's turn to touch.

4.2: Freeze Dance

This activity requires no resources at all! Play some songs in an

Self-Control Skills at Home for Kids

open area. Kids will dance when the song is playing, but when it stops, they will freeze! Let children maintain a yoga pose while they freeze if you want to make it harder.

4.3: Identify Your Anger

Children make choices that they eventually come to regret. We could say or do hurtful or accidental things when we're angry or irritated. When your child gets angry next time, try this practice to assess how you could have done things differently. Ask the child to locate three instances when they have gotten angry and afterward regretted it. By reflecting on the past, we become better aware of how things are going and whether they are doing well or not. In order to help youngsters develop good moods and emotions, it can be helpful to give an example of how they might respond differently. Given below is a worksheet, to let you write your anger story:

Identify Your Anger

What happened?	How could I have acted differently?

Self-Control Skills at Home for Kids

4.4: My Anger Bubbles

An angry idea in each bubble should make you take back your lost control. For problems that cause you more distress, use the more giant bubbles; for mild irritants, use the smaller bubbles.

My Anger Bubbles

Self-Control Skills at Home for Kids

4.5: Follow the Shapes

In this activity, you will help your kid to draw shapes. You will show them the shape by drawing it on paper, and they will follow it. The kids will have to try their best to draw the required shapes accurately. This activity enhances their drawing skills and helps to invest their time in the drawing.

4.6: Simon Says

This activity emphasizes the both; self-control and concentration skills. Children must have the self-control to prevent themselves if "Simon" will not really say to do something; thus, they must pay close attention to hear what he wants to do. Pass orders like "Simon says to place your hands on your heads" and "Simon says balance solely on a single foot." Then, check if they can follow along after you replace one that doesn't start with "Simon says." Then you may change it up and let the kids take the lead.

4.7: Warning Signals

There can be many reasons to become extremely aggressive. When you are in rage sometimes, you can't control yourself and explode at the other person. Similarly, when kids get aggressive, parents should not take the strict actions immediately. Instead of this, you can calm your child and engage them with the activity as provided below. Instruct you child to write some warning signs which they will use, when they become aggressive. Whenever they will become aggressive and can't control

70

themselves to blow up, this activity will remind them all the written warning signs. You can use the worksheet given below to do this activity.

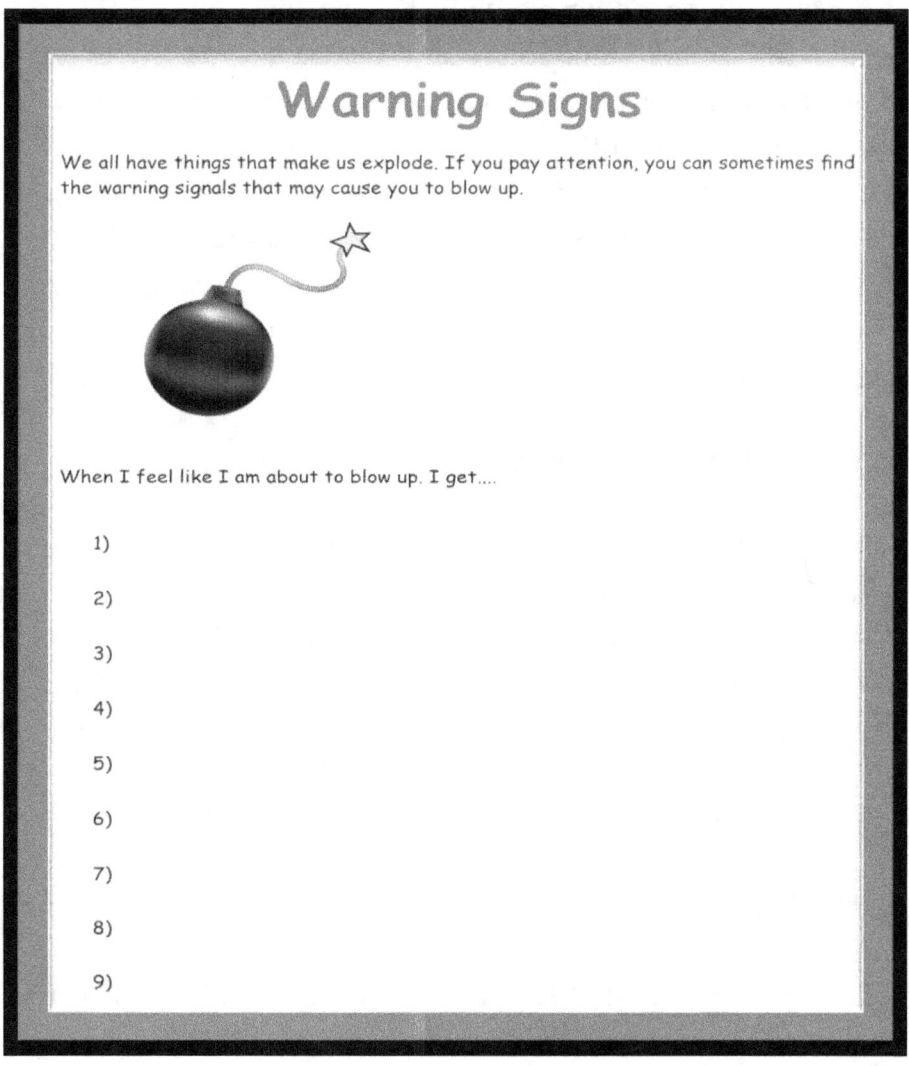

Warning Signs

We all have things that make us explode. If you pay attention, you can sometimes find the warning signals that may cause you to blow up.

When I feel like I am about to blow up. I get....

1)

2)

3)

4)

5)

6)

7)

8)

9)

Self-Control Skills at Home for Kids

4.8: Jenga

This activity is my favorite due to its ideal balance of both order and disorder (ideal for those kids who truly need to learn self-control!). Every moment a child takes a block out of the tower while they are playing, you should tell them to practice caution. Your chances of winning increase as you become more careful and attentive. The entire activity becomes a model for self-control in everyday life, making it a highly entertaining and engaging approach to learning self-control. Things can unravel if you are not careful. Consider taking your time, pause, and move cautiously once you have thought over the things. You can perform this activity with your child over and over again.

4.9: The Obstacle Course

This amusing obstacle course activity for kids is a great method to encourage collaboration and interpersonal skills in addition to self-control skills like balancing and coordination. Below is the worksheet for this activity in which your child has to write about the obstacles he is facing to control his or her anger or rage. In this way, your child learns about many obstacles that they face at that moment, and they will work on these.

4.10: Stick to the Clapping Pattern

This is a great activity to start off a session or end one. The leader begins to clap repeatedly in a rhythm. One kid then extends the process after all kids have followed it. The kids must follow the

72

modifications in the pattern. Try to modify the pattern as many times as you can.

Chapter 5: "Become Aware of the Reality"

Typically, when we consider stress, we only consider its drawbacks. Feelings of "major source of stress!" come to our mind. A major incident or circumstance can throw someone's life out of balance. When something is bothering a child too much it results in stress and this stress creates extreme anxiety. Stress frequently originates from circumstances that are out of our control. Stress levels have a lot to do with control.

We benefit from some stress because it gives us the strength we need to get up and begin our days. Stress that is excessive, ongoing or that is experienced without the assistance of loved ones is seen as poisonous. Stress that is harmful makes us ill and miserable. Stress can affect a child's growth, emotions, and attitude. Kids who are stressed often complain of having stomach issues, anxiety, difficulties sleeping, angry outbursts, and even diseases or illnesses. Kids who are under stress may also exhibit certain patterns, including lashing out, losing mastery of previously learned skills, and becoming clingy or distant.

5.1: Observing and Accepting your Child's worries

Kids occasionally reject experiences that feel unfamiliar or difficult. However, trying new things that really are safe and appropriate for their ages helps them to develop. They can develop their abilities and courage with each new adventure.

74

Parents may support their children and teenagers in embracing change without allowing fear to hold them back.

Give them your Time: **Perform this each day, even if it is just a little while. Spend time doing activities that you really enjoy. Take a stroll, prepare food, eat, play, or simply relax. Find methods to laugh and grin as a group. This maintains your relationship solid and everlasting and it provides opportunities for kids to open out simply.**

Inquire About their Thoughts: **Help children identify their thoughts and feelings. Occasionally they may not have much to say. Additionally, kids may occasionally not want to express what is in their thoughts. However, let children know you are always willing to listen and converse.**

Patiently Pay Attention: **Give your undivided attention when children or teenagers want to speak. Allow them time to express their feelings and opinions in words. Inquire further to learn more. Be cautious when dispensing advice. Let them open up. Be calm and take in the things they have to share.**

Validate: Let children know that you comprehend. Tell them it's alright to have their feelings. Convey them that their emotions are normal. Avoid saying things like, "There's really nothing to worry about." Children may believe that their feelings are inappropriate in light of this. Instead, gently listen to them and embrace their feelings. Kids find it simpler to share as a result.

75

Self-Control Skills at Home for Kids

Encourage them: Encourage children to consider their options. Encourage them to feel capable. Avoid intervening to resolve their problems. Instead, encourage children to consider what they can achieve. Assist with their smart suggestions. Discuss it in detail together. Tell them of moments when they experimented and succeeded. If assistance is required, offer it.

Support in their Practice: Help kids to learn new things whenever you can. Let them exercise one step at a time as they move toward their objective. Celebrate each achievement.

Honor your Kid: Honor your kid's effort and development. Let them understand that you were proud of what they accomplished or said. Encourage them to have high hopes. Ask your youngster to share their positive experiences and upcoming plans. Inquire about the positive events that occurred throughout their day. Educate them about your day's highlights as well. Inform them that while talking about anxieties is acceptable, concentrating more on the positive moments is also beneficial.

Calming and Consolation: Kids occasionally may have overloaded stress. Talking it out won't likely help under those circumstances. The ability to be calm and empathize might be more beneficial. Inform them that you are there to support them as they navigate through life's challenges. Teach them how to breathe deeply and slowly to relax their thoughts and body.

Self-Control Skills at Home for Kids

5.2: Some Impulse Control Techniques

According to studies, ineffective impulse control is associated with bad decision-making, the onset of mental health issues, and poor decision-making. Therefore, the more self-control your kid develops, the less likely it is that he would act or say anything that could harm them or any others, and the more possible it is that he will have good mental health.

- *Teach your Kid to Identify Feelings*

Impulsivity is more prevalent among kids who don't comprehend or understand how to express their emotions well.

77

Self-Control Skills at Home for Kids

A child that is unable to express his anger verbally may hit to do so. Or a kid who is unable to express his sadness may shout or throw other tantrums. Encourage your child to identify their emotions so they can express themselves to you verbally rather than physically. Start by showing your youngster the names of common emotions, such as anger, sadness, excitement, surprise, worry, and fear. Make sure kids understand that while feeling angry is acceptable, hitting, kicking, or yelling at others while being furious is not.

- *Your Child Reviews the Instructions*

When children don't listen to instructions, they can act impulsively. This is especially true of children with ADHD. Make sure they're really listening to help them maintain their course. If not, they can rush into action before you have finished your directions while you are still speaking. Additionally, try to keep the number of stages in the instructions to a minimum. Your child's individual ability to follow complicated instructions should also be taken into account.

- *Develop Problem-Solving Techniques*

Even if it sounds easy to come up with answers, problem-solving is one of the best methods for impulse control. Teach your youngster that there are various approaches to problem-solving and that it would be wise to consider various options before making a decision. Enable them to know which potential solutions are far more likely to be beneficial after helping them

78

find potential solutions. They can learn to think things through before acting, with some practice.

- *Teach the Control of Rage*

Impulsive tantrums may result from a low tolerance for anger. Giving your child the tools to control their aggression can enable them to express their feelings in a healthy manner. Give them specific techniques, such as exhaling deeply or walking home to waste off some energy. Even better put up a bag of relaxation techniques to assist them in developing calmness. Without acting rashly, teaching kids how to control their emotions and make better decisions is important.

- *Specify Household Regulations*

Establish specific norms and provide justifications for them. Since your kid will know what behaviors are expected of them, giving them a framework and standards can help them develop better impulse control.

- *Set an Example for Others*

By observing you, your youngster will pick up a lot regarding impulse control. Set a good example of how to wait quietly and accept deferred pleasure. Speaking aloud to yourself will assist your child in learning how to create an inner monologue that will enable them to control their urges.

79

5.3: Your Child doesn't Have to be Perfect

As a parent, it's your responsibility to understand your child and accept them with all their flaws. One of life's toughest task is raising a child, yet it's also the one for which you can feel to be least qualified. Using these nine child-raising suggestions, you may feel better as a parent.

- *Encourage your Kid's Self-Esteem*

Children begin to form a sense of identity when they perceive themselves through their parents' eyes. Your children are observing everything you say and did, such as your expressions and body language. Above all else, your behaviors and words as a parent have an effect on how children build self-esteem. Appreciate them for their accomplishments, does not matter how little they are, will make children happy. Allowing kids to complete tasks individually will make children feel capable and powerful. Kids will feel useless if they are subjected to negative remarks or comparisons that are not favorable to them.

Avoid using foul language or negative comments. Just like physical attacks, remarks like "*What a foolish thing you are doing!*" can hurt. Take care of your words precisely and be kind to others. Tell your children that even though you disapprove of their behavior, you always love them and understand that everyone makes several errors in their life.

Self-Control Skills at Home for Kids

- *Notice Children Doing Good*

Did you ever consider how regularly in one day you behave negatively with your kids? You might find that you tend to criticize far more than you do to praise. A more effective technique is to catch kids doing something right: "*You cleaned your bedroom even though you weren't asked — that's fantastic!*" or "*I observed how kind you were when I saw you enjoying with your sibling.*" Over time, these comments will have a greater positive impact on behavior than those regular sanctions.

Make it a goal to find a good thing to say every day. Be generous with your compliments; they often come back to you in the form of warmth, smiles, and encouraging words. You'll soon observe that you are behaving more in line with your desired conduct.

- *Establish Boundaries and Apply your Discipline Consistently*

Every household needs order. Through regulation, kids are meant to understand how to make good decision and develop self-control in them. They may test the limits you establish for children, but they need those limits to grow up to be mature, responsible adults. By abiding by set house rules, kids can develop self-control and better understand your expectations. One rule could be: No TV until completion of homework.

You might choose to implement a system that starts with a warning and then punishment or privilege reductions. A

81

common error made by parents is their incapacity to administer punishment. Children cannot be disciplined in just one-day while being ignored the next by the parents. People learn what to expect when there is consistency.

- *Spend Time with Your Children*

It might be difficult for parents and kids to sit down to a family meal or even to spend quality time together. I don't think anything would, though, attract to them more. If you want to share a meal with your youngster, try to get up 15 minutes sooner than usual. If you want to go for a picnic with your child after supper, load the dishwasher first. Children commonly misbehave or lash out when their parents don't give them the attention they want since they believe they'll be caught.

Many parents love planning time to spend with their kids as a family. Each week, schedule a dinner for your family, and allow the kids to help you decide how to spend your precious time. Find alternative means of communication; you can think about hiding a special note or item in your kid's backpack. Teenagers don't need as much attention from parents as younger kids do. There are fewer opportunities for children and parents to spend time together, so parents should make an effort to be available when their child indicates a desire to communicate or participate in family activities. Attending football games, celebrations, and other activities with your child demonstrates your concern for them and makes it possible for you to form everlasting bonds between them and their classmates. The simple things parents do

82

with their kids, like baking cookies and playing games, will be remembered by the kids.

- *Act as a Good Example*

Kids learn a lot about way of living by observing their parents. Younger kids are more receptive to your cues. When you lose your temper or start screaming in front of your child, think about this: *Do you wish for them to behave in this way when they're angry?* Remember that your kids are always watching you. Studies show that children who are aggressive usually have an aggressive grownup at home. Teach your kids how to act in a tolerant, compassionate, fair, generous, and understanding manner. Be a selfless person and don't seek rewards while doing something for others. Above all else, always remember to treat your kids the way you want them to treat you.

- *Prioritize Communication*

Even if their parents might be doing something, kids are not supposed to copy them. Like grownups, kids seek and anticipate solutions. If we are unwilling to take the effort to clarify to children, they will begin to doubt our views and reasons. Make your expectations clear. If you see a problem, talk about it with your child, let them know what you think about it, and encourage them to assist you in fixing it. If you can, mention the outcomes. Present alternatives and recommend changes. Pay attention to your children's recommendations as well. Children who participate in decision-making are more likely to carry them out.

83

Self-Control Skills at Home for Kids

- *Be Adaptable and Prepared to Change your Parenting Approach*

If you constantly feel "let down" by your kid's development, it's probable that you possess high expectations from them. Parents with "must" attitudes might find it helpful to research the issue more or speak with specialists in early childhood development. Since children's surroundings influence their behaviors, changing the surroundings may alter that behavior. As a result, neither of you may feel as annoyed. As your child gets older, you'll need to gradually change your parenting style. Over the next year or two, your child's current behaviors are likely to end. Kids typically seek to their friends for role models rather than their parents. However, as you give your child more responsibility, continue to offer them guidance, encouragement, and appropriate consequences. Additionally, take advantage of whatever chance you get to connect.

- *Demonstrate your Love and Respect*

As a parent, it is your responsibility to discipline and guide your kids. When it is necessary to communicate to your kid, try to avoid blaming, criticizing, or taking sides because these behaviors can result in anger and self-esteem problems. Even when you are disciplining your kids, try to remain positive and loving. Tell them that your affection will always be there, although you expect and predict better results in the future.

Self-Control Skills at Home for Kids

- *Be Aware of Your Own Wants and Boundaries*

Let's admit it, you are an imperfect parent. You have benefits and drawbacks as the home leader. Identify your positive qualities and declare, "*I am truthful and compassionate.*" Make a commitment to yourself to get better: "*I must be more consistent with rules.*" Focus on the issues that require the greatest attention rather than tackling everything at once. When you're tired out, admit it. Spend some time doing things you enjoy doing instead of parenting. If you put your needs first, you are not self-centered. It implies that you care for your own wellbeing, which is another essential characteristic for providing a good example for your children.

Self-Control Skills at Home for Kids

A Final Positive Note

As kids enter middle school, parents frequently lose interest in their kids' lives. However, your child requires as much of your affection and concern as he did when he was younger — if not more. Your kid's best defense as he matures and develops is a positive association with you as well as with other grownups. Though the brain develops significantly during the initial five years of one's life, some areas of the brain grow more gradually than others. Nevertheless, even in toddlers, certain parts of executive function, such as the capacity to concentrate, maintain memory skills, and self-regulate activities, can be strengthened via explicit training, encouragement, and practice. Parents and preschool teachers should interact with young kids to encourage the development of these skills because there is an excellent reason to do so. Children who demonstrate self-controlled behaviors go on to experience greater academic performance and are significantly more likely to resist from dangerous behaviors in teens than their classmates who struggle with self-control.

Children naturally have highs and lows, just like the rest of us. Children can start to realize that they are able to take control of their emotions when they receive kind attention from concerned grownups during their angry phases. Identify when kids are upset or ignored, engage them in conversation about their thoughts without being judgmental, and ask them how they may handle them in a way that doesn't damage anybody else.

Self-Control Skills at Home for Kids

Moreover, even though it might be challenging, try to control your rage when it comes to correcting your children. Be forceful and direct instead of being soft. When a youngster is having a tantrum, remain calm and explain that inappropriate behaviors like screaming, tantrums, and loud noises will result in punishments. Your behavior will demonstrate that kids can't win by throwing tantrums. If your kid starts to cry at the supermarket, even if you've discussed why you didn't purchase candy, avoid the temptation to give in. This will show your child that their rage was inappropriate and unproductive.

Consider discussing classroom dynamics and proper behavior standards with your child's instructors as well. Inquire as to whether problem-solving is presented or practiced in schools. Be an example of self-control. If you find yourself in a frustrating position in the presence of your children, explain to them the reason you're upset before going into alternative remedies. For instance, if you lose your cards, instead of feeling outraged, tell your children and have them help you look for them. If they don't show up, move on to something helpful. Demonstrate how to manage challenging circumstances using appropriate emotional regulation and problem-solving skills.

Self-Control Skills at Home for Kids

www.ingramcontent.com/pod-product-compliance
Lightning Source LLC
Chambersburg PA
CBHW071114120626
46546CB00003B/1331